Original title:
Rhododendron Rhymes

Copyright © 2025 Creative Arts Management OÜ
All rights reserved.

Author: Nathaniel Blackwood
ISBN HARDBACK: 978-1-80566-693-6
ISBN PAPERBACK: 978-1-80566-978-4

Lush Lines

In the garden, green and bright,
Flowers giggle, what a sight!
Petals dance with playful glee,
Nature's jesters, wild and free.

Bees buzz by in silly flight,
Wiggly worms keep up the fright.
Laughter blooms in every hue,
As landscape sings its merry tune.

Whispers of Wildflowers

In the meadow, secrets play,
Buttercups winking at the day.
Tulips tease with swaying sway,
Petals whisper, come and play!

Daisies giggle, oh so round,
Sunflowers spinning, dizzy bound.
A dandelion takes a turn,
Puffing wishes, watch them burn.

The Poetry of Growth

Little sprouts with mighty dreams,
Reaching high past sunlit beams.
Bumblebees with merry cheer,
Join the party, don't you fear!

With each sprinkle, life's a tease,
Grasshoppers dance with ease.
Nature's book is funny lore,
Each page turning, wanting more.

Rhymes among the Roses

In a patch of rosy bloom,
Thorns are casting lots of gloom.
But petals laugh, they wear their pride,
In fragrant jokes, they all confide.

Ladybugs share silly tales,
As naughty winds blow funny gales.
Roses blush as sunshine plays,
They sway and giggle through the days.

Enchanted Blooms

In a garden of giggles, blooms are bright,
They dance with the breeze, a silly sight.
A bee wears a bow tie, struts with glee,
While butterflies giggle, 'Come play with me!'

Pansies tell tales, with petals so wide,
While daisies sneak whispers, trying to hide.
The tulips are twerking, oh what a scene,
In this floral party, the silliest green!

Lullabies of the Flora

Under the moon, the flowers hum,
Their lullabies make sleepy bees numb.
The daisies snore soft, dreaming of sun,
While violets chuckle, 'We can't be outdone!'

Roses for jokes, with thorns that tease,
Tulips fall over, just laughing with ease.
In the quiet night, the garden's a show,
With petals a-flutter, putting on a glow!

Echoes of Springtime

Spring's here with a laugh, oh what a sound,
The crocus start prancing, spinning around.
Chirping little sparrows, oh what a cheer,
Singing silly songs that all the buds hear!

The lilacs all wink, with a hint of jest,
Each blossom a prankster, they love to invest.
In this vibrant chaos, the flowers collide,
With humor and laughter, they bloom with pride!

Vibrant Verses Untold

Bright blooms on a canvas, colors collide,
Sunflowers chuckle, wearing smiles with pride.
The garden's a circus, a joyous parade,
With blooming tomfoolery in every shade!

Petunias play tricks, while lilies sing loud,
In this floral drama, let's join the crowd.
So grab all your friends, come join the spree,
Where laughter and petals are wild and free!

Imagery in Bloom

In a garden where colors collide,
The petals all dance with pride.
A purple guy tried to lead,
But tripped on a bumblebee's greed.

The roses all giggled with glee,
As the daisies joined in for a spree.
The tulips proclaimed with a shout,
'We're in bloom, let's party about!'

The Blooming Troupe

A troupe of blossoms, silly and bright,
Performed for the bugs in the fading light.
The sunflowers spun with flaring delight,
While violets bobbed, trying to take flight.

The daffodils danced, all in a row,
With crocus clowns putting on a show.
The lilacs fell over, laughing so loud,
As butterflies cheered for their flowery crowd.

Swaying in the Zephyr

In the breeze, a twist and a twirl,
Petals spun like a wild, crazy whirl.
A tulip said, 'Just look at me!'
As it spun right into a bumblebee.

The lilacs hung on for dear life,
While pansies watched—oh, what a strife!
But with a giggle and all in jest,
They declared, 'Together, we are the best!'

The Colors of Harmony

A rainbow came down for a plunge,
And borrowed some petals for a fun lunge.
"Mismatched is the new style," it cried,
With a feather and a leaf, it glorified.

The tulips wore hats of dandelion fluff,
While marigolds giggled, "Is this enough?"
With colors so wacky, they painted the sky,
In a floral fiesta, oh my, oh my!

Fragrant Fables

In gardens where the colors pop,
The flowers dance, they never stop.
With twists and turns and giggles loud,
They tease the bees, they draw a crowd.

The blooms wear hats, so wacky bright,
They sway and sway, what a delight.
A bloom once said, with fragrant cheer,
"Why not wear pants? Let's start a smear!"

The Annual Anthology

Each spring we gather, what a sight,
With blooms in bloom and hearts so light.
A contest here, a joke or two,
Who can tell the funniest dew?

The petals laugh, they shake and twist,
"I'm not a rose!" one daisy hissed.
From puns to jests, the fun won't cease,
As blooms unite, they laugh in peace.

Blooms Under Moonlight

Under the moon, the petals play,
They whisper secrets, night and day.
"Oh look, a gnome!" a hyacinth squealed,
With giggles loud, the night revealed.

They twirl and leap, a colorful show,
As stars above wink soft and slow.
Who knew a flower could be so spry?
They jest and jibe beneath the sky.

Lyrical Blossoms

The blossoms gather for a tune,
In soft sunlight, beneath the moon.
With petals ruffled, voices sweet,
They croon to bugs on tiny feet.

One flower stumbles, then starts to rhyme,
"I swear I bloomed here just in time!"
With laughter shared, they fill the air,
A symphony of petals rare.

The Language of Leaves

In the garden, leaves chatter,
Whispering tales of nature's matter.
They gossip about the weather's cheer,
Swaying gently from year to year.

Tales of sun and tales of rain,
Of every bulging root and vein.
The trees listen, nodding their heads,
While rabbits giggle and dance in their beds.

Nature's Kaleidoscope

Colors collide in a vibrant show,
As petals twirl and giggle below.
The blues and reds in a playful race,
Each bloom trying to win the best face.

Bees start humming a secret tune,
While butterflies prance like they'd won a boon.
Every hue has a story to spin,
In this laughter, everyone wins!

Secrets of the Shrubs

The bushes whisper, 'Can you keep it?,'
A secret about the wind's tiny trip.
They shake with laughter, branches a-jig,
As squirrels ponder, grinning so big.

In the shade, they plot their next move,
With shadows that dance and cleverly groove.
Who knew such mischief lives in green,
When no one's watching, they're quite the scene!

A Floral Symphony

Flowers gather for a concert grand,
With tulips on drums and daisies in band.
They sing about sunshine and rain,
While crickets and frogs join in the refrain.

With petals waving like fans in delight,
They put on a show in the soft evening light.
In the bloomers' world, the fun never ends,
With each note played, nature's best friends!

The Dance of the Petals

The petals twist and spin with glee,
In a breeze, they dance with me.
A swirl of colors, pink and red,
They leap and bounce, no time for dread.

They giggle softly, rustle loud,
Swinging, bending, a floral crowd.
With every flutter, laughs ignite,
A petal party, what a sight!

Nature's Colorful Poetry

Look at those flowers, wearing their hats,
Bouncing around, even chatting with cats.
Each bloom has a quirk, a tale to share,
Silly little whispers float in the air.

Colors collide in a playful twist,
Even bees can't resist the floral tryst.
A poem unfolds in the garden's cheer,
Scribbles in petals, oh, come near!

Botanical Ballads

Singing songs of sun and rain,
The daisies chuckle; they're never plain.
Hummingbirds swoop with a wink and laugh,
Every leaf joins in, a botanical half.

Petal troubadours strum in the breeze,
Each note a giggle that lives with ease.
Nature's orchestra, no need for a tent,
A melody of blooms, frolicking, unbent!

Floral Reverie

In a dream of colors bright and bold,
Petal pranks and tales are told.
A dandelion juggles in a lawn,
While sunflowers cheer, their laughter drawn.

Tulips trip on their silky stems,
Competing in dance like tiny gems.
With every giggle, they twist and sway,
In this floral dreamland, we all play!

Whispering Blossoms

In the garden, blooms do dance,
With petals bright, they take their chance.
They giggle low, they sway and twirl,
A secret language in a whirl.

A bee buzzes by, wearing a crown,
He's got his shades; he won't back down.
These flowers gossip, oh what a plight,
"Did you see that bug? He's quite a sight!"

Garden Serenade

Beneath the sky, the colors sing,
A melody made by spring's sweet fling.
With lazy bees and lazy hints,
The flowers sway and break old mince.

In tune they laugh, in rhythm they sway,
"Who knew that thorns could dance this way?"
Each blossom hums a jolly tune,
While bunnies bop to the bouncing moon.

Shades of Flora

Petals in pink, and green in sprawl,
They throw a party, come one, come all.
Each leaf a joke, each bud a jest,
Nature's humor, it's simply the best.

In the corner, the daisies tall,
Claim they're the stars of this floral ball.
But shy violets hold a witty spat,
"Don't forget us! We're where it's at!"

The Symphony of Stems

Stems all lined in a cheerful row,
Conducting laughter as breezes blow.
A gentle rustle, the leaves take flight,
Turning the day from dull to bright.

Here comes the rose, with stories grand,
Telling the tale of the petal band.
With every bloom, the laughter swells,
In leafy whispers, a tale that tells.

Wildflower Dreams

In a field of blooms so bright,
The bees dance with sheer delight.
A squirrel wears a flower crown,
Thinking he's the king of town.

Laughter echoes through the grass,
As butterflies go skipping past.
Each petal holds a giggle sound,
In this garden, joy is found.

The daisies gossip, oh so loud,
While tulips prance, they're quite the crowd.
Sunflowers grin at every joke,
As vines twist up and playful poke.

Underneath the shady tree,
The plants sing songs, so carefree.
With vibrant hues and silly schemes,
We bloom and burst with wildflower dreams.

Harmony Among the Blossoms

In the garden where they meet,
Petunias know how to dance on feet.
Roses roll their eyes in spite,
They think they're such a pretty sight.

Lilies laugh at fragrant tales,
While daisies tell of epic fails.
A marigold attempts to rap,
But ends up in a pollen nap.

The violets wear their classy gear,
While sunflowers shout, "Hey, look here!"
The blossoms joke and tease and play,
In harmony, they spend the day.

They make a list of silly pranks,
And plot to prank the garden tanks.
Underneath the sun's embrace,
There's laughter blooming in this place.

Gardens of Memory

In the plot where flowers laugh,
Old memories bloom, a sunny path.
A daffodil tells tales of cheer,
While nearby, a butterfly appears.

Each petal shares a funny tale,
Of wind-blown trips and fateful gales.
The roses chuckle at their thorn,
Saying, "Beauty can be worn and torn!"

The snapdragons play a bursty game,
With puns that always sound the same.
While daisies twist their cheerful heads,
They giggle at the stories spread.

As memory drifts like summer air,
The garden sings without a care.
With every laugh and every cheer,
The flowers bloom, year after year.

The Color of Poetry

In a palette bright and wild,
Colors dance like a joyful child.
Green and gold, a playful clash,
In this garden, words just splash.

The reds declare, "We are the best!"
The blues respond, "We pass the test!"
Yellow giggles, "I'm pure delight!"
While purples plot a fancy flight.

The hues collide in playful fights,
Sprouting rhymes on sunny nights.
Daffodils with smiles that gleam,
Are scribbling thoughts, oh what a theme!

Each bloom a stanza, each leaf a rhyme,
In gardens where we lose all time.
So grab a brush, don't be shy,
Let's paint this poetry and let it fly!

Blooms Beneath the Moon

Under the moon, they twirl and sway,
Petals giggle, come what may.
A dance of colors, bright and bold,
Each one tells a joke untold.

The flowers cackle, oh what a scene,
Bouncing under silver sheen.
Whispers of pollen, quick and spry,
As bees buzz by and sigh, oh my!

Laughter echoes in the night air,
In this garden, no need to despair.
With roots deep set in playful ease,
They tease the stars, they tease the breeze.

So when you glance at blooms aglow,
Remember the jokes that they bestow.
For laughter bubbles where blossoms bloom,
A funny tale beneath the moon.

Nature's Echoing Ballad

In the meadow, where songbirds chirp,
The flowers join in, with quite a burp.
They bounce along with each merry note,
And wilt with laughter on the floor of the mote.

Bees accidentally take a wrong turn,
Into the petals where they all yearn.
"Hey, watch it!" the daisies yell in glee,
As blooms erupt in a riot of spree!

Swaying to rhythms only they hear,
They crack up loudly, not showing fear.
With such a tune, who could stay sad?
Even the thorns join in, though it's mad!

So stroll through this symphony, catch the fun,
Nature's humor shines, bright as the sun.
Let laughter carry, let worries unfurl,
In this whimsical, floral world!

Blossoms and Boundaries

Around the edges, flowers friend,
Wondering where their ruckus will end.
"Stay in your lane!" the tulips shout,
But the daisies just dance about.

"No weeds allowed!" the roses declare,
As pansies giggle with flair.
But in this patch, rules take a dive,
Every few blooms feels quite alive!

They plot and they plan mischief so sly,
With petals flapping like flags up high.
"Who needs boundaries? Let's cross the lines!"
With laughter uproarious through curvy vines!

So if you find this garden of jest,
Know it's where blooms put rules to the test.
For in the laughter that flows like streams,
Are petals living their wildest dreams!

The Dance of Color

A twirl of hues, a burst of cheer,
The sunflowers nod, "Come over here!"
Amidst the vibrant blooms, they prance,
In petals soft, they take a chance.

Colorful rhymes in the springtime play,
Each blossom teasing in a floral ballet.
"Oh look at me!" the lilacs call,
As they trip over the hyacinth wall.

With laughter ringing, they form a line,
Dancing together, feeling just fine.
Every shade and every tone,
Brings a smile; they're never alone!

So come join in this colorful whirl,
Where laughter blooms in a joyous swirl.
In the garden of giggles, life's a spree,
With petals singing in harmony!

Palettes of Petals

In gardens bright, the petals dance,
With colors bold, they take a chance.
A purple bloom, a yellow stare,
They giggle softly in the air.

The flowers wear their hats so high,
As bees come buzzing, oh so spry.
A petal jaunt, a fragrant spree,
Who knew they'd have such comedy?

Their skirts of green, a leafy twist,
In sunshine, they can't help but twist.
The daisies laugh, the roses frown,
In this wild garden comedy town.

So come and join this petal play,
Where blooms would smile the day away.
A palette here, a palette there,
The flowers jest, without a care.

Sonnet in Bloom

A flower's wink, a leaf's sly grin,
They prance about, let games begin.
"Hey, look at me, I'm quite the catch!"
The lilacs scream, the violets snatch.

A tulip trips, a poppy rolls,
Each petal filled with jokes and goals.
"Do I smell funny?" asks the rose,
With laughter shared, the garden glows.

In fragrant air, their secrets blend,
A giggling bud, a laughing friend.
The blooms unite, both bold and bright,
In this sonnet, all will delight.

As petals tickle, the bees all cheer,
"Your puns have bloomed, we love you dear!"
Let nature's humor find its way,
And fill our hearts with blooms that play.

Ode to the Outrageous

Oh blossoms wild, with tricks so loud,
In nature's court, they laugh so proud.
The dandelions joke, "We're the stars!"
As daisies join with giggles in bars.

The tulips boast of style and flair,
While petunias sway in fragrant air.
A daffodil shouts, "I'm gold and bright!"
In this comic garden, what a sight!

Their shades collide in riotous cheer,
A bumblebee appears, oh dear!
"Did you just hear that pun?" he buzzed,
And off he flew in pollen fuzzed.

An ode, a toast, to blooms so free,
In outrageous hues, they dance with glee.
So let us laugh with flowers about,
In this garden's joy, we'll roam throughout.

The Elegance of Pink

Oh hues of rose, so bright and fine,
In springtime's glow, they twist and twine.
"Look at me sway!" the pinks all sing,
As laughter flows, it keeps on springing.

A petal fuss, a blushing face,
They twirl and whirl in happy grace.
With fragrant giggles, they flirt and play,
In this garden, joy finds its way.

The cherry blossoms cause a buzz,
"Are we not the finest?" they all fuss.
In soft pink hues, they prance around,
With elegance that knows no bounds.

So here's to pink, with laughter rife,
In every bloom, there's joy and life.
As petals wobble, a charming wink,
In nature's dance, we stop and think.

Songs of the Mountain

In the hills, where flowers sway,
A bee got lost, took a holiday.
He danced with petals, oh what a sight,
Buzzing tunes till the fall of night.

The rocks all chuckled, the trees joined in,
A butterfly laughed, then slipped on a pin.
They planted jokes in the soft, warm air,
Nature's giggles, beyond compare.

The sunshine winked, the clouds wore hats,
A squirrel cracked jokes while loving the chats.
With each bright color, laughter would bloom,
In this mountain garden, joy filled the room.

Blooming in Abandon

Petals party, what a wild bash,
With fairies drinking dew from a flash.
They twirled in circles, under the sun,
A flower went home, but forgot how to run.

Bees wore shades, sipping sweet tea,
While a ladybug played the ukulele with glee.
In this floral fest, no worries to track,
They danced till their stems simply fell back.

A snail on a swing, just taking it slow,
Caterpillars grooved, putting on a show.
The garden erupted in laughter and cheer,
As petals rejoiced, oh what a year!

Petal Dreams at Dusk

As twilight fell, the flowers sat tight,
Sharing their secrets under the night.
A rose told tales of her flirty past,
While tulips teased, "Should we dye our grass?"

Daisies whispered, "Who's got the best scent?"
While violets plotted a prank, oh what a bent!
An owl hooted, chiming in late,
"Keep quiet you blooms, you're tempting fate!"

They giggled and chuckled, with dreams in the air,
Each petal a poet, shedding all care.
In the garden at dusk, mischief arose,
With laughter and dreams, anything goes!

The Essence of Eden

In Eden's heart, where humor grew,
A cactus complained, "I need a shoe!"
The roses replied with petals so bright,
"Let's wrap you up, you're a funny sight!"

A tulip thought, "Let's throw a bash!"
And invited all critters, oh what a splash!
The planning went wild, no detail was small,
As daisies sketched maps on the garden wall.

A robin wore glasses, a snail wore a tie,
While worms formed a conga line passing by.
Every blossom burst into sing-along fun,
Creating a circus, oh how they run!

Blossoms in the Breeze

A flower sneezed, oh what a sight,
Its pollen danced, took off in flight.
A bee wore shades, thought it a show,
Buzzed in tune, stealing the flow.

Sprinklers laughed, they splashed a stream,
While butterflies hatched a silly dream.
The tulips waltzed, in dresses bright,
Teasing the daisies, 'We'll outshine you tonight!'

A grumpy gnome took a sip of tea,
Accidentally spilled, oh dear me!
The sun chuckled, its rays a tease,
As petals giggled in the playful breeze.

So let us prance in garden's play,
Where blooms unite in their own ballet.
With humor tucked in every stem,
A flowered laugh, oh what a gem!

Petals and Whispers

Whispers beneath the leafy green,
Petals gossip, oh so keen.
A bumblebee, within earshot,
Joined the joke, oh what a plot!

The daisies whispered, 'Let's have fun!'
Buttercups giggled in the sun.
A rolling stone named Ivy said,
'Keep it quiet, or I'll lose my head!'

Hummingbirds chimed in with a trill,
While snails slid down, not in a thrill.
The daisies plotted, 'Let's dance tonight,'
And off they twirled, all sparkly and bright.

So gather round, in blooms' embrace,
With laughter echoing, it's our space.
In this garden of mischief and cheer,
Let's dance with our petals, let's persevere!

The Garden's Serenade

In a garden where the laughter grows,
With petals flapping like a rose.
Crickets crooned, a serenade,
While flowers twirled in the grand parade.

A sunflower wore a silly grin,
Boasting it was the best in the bin.
But daisies rolled their eyes in jest,
'We've got the charm, and you know the rest!'

A ladybug played the tambourine,
While mint leaves danced, fresh and green.
The soil chuckled with every tune,
As seeds made wishes 'neath the moon.

So let the garden echo our song,
Where colors burst and laughs prolong.
In this fiesta of blooms and cheer,
Every whisper blossoms, drawing near!

Colors of the Heart

Colors splashed! Oh what a spree,
The violets laughed, 'Come dance with me!'
With reds and yellows, a palette bright,
Painting joy from morning to night.

An artist's brush planted a frown,
As marigolds wore a royal crown.
'Who's the fairest?' they teased and pranced,
While butterflies around them danced.

Petals swayed to a jazzy beat,
And daisies tapped their tiny feet.
Every hue found a buddy near,
In colors of laughter, we hold dear.

So come together, let's mix and blend,
With a canvas of joy that won't pretend.
For in every color, a giggle is found,
In this garden of laughter, we are all bound!

Blossoms in the Breeze

Petals dance with laughter bright,
They swirl and twirl in gleeful flight.
Buzzing bees join in the fun,
Wiggle, giggle, under the sun.

Squirrels peek with curious eyes,
As flowers bloom and whisper sighs.
A breeze tickles, a leaf takes chase,
Nature's joke is this silly race.

Dandelions puff, they laugh so loud,
Tickling toes of the joyous crowd.
Blossoms bow in playful cheer,
While butterflies shed all their fear.

The garden's stage, a grand display,
Where blooms perform the liveliest play.
Each flower a star, unique, so fine,
In this wild show of colors divine.

Echoes of the Evergreen

Tall trees chuckle with their leaves,
As squirrels hide 'neath woven eaves.
An acorn drops, a thudding sound,
The woodland whispers, all around.

Branches sway, a comedic waltz,
Nature's humor, it never faults.
Birds chirp jokes, a feathered crew,
Their giggles echo through the blue.

A deer trips on a twisted root,
And laughs erupt in leafy pursuit.
The mossy ground is soft and neat,
For nature's jesters at their feet.

With every breeze, the trees all sway,
Telling tales of a playful day.
Leaves exchange gossip of delight,
As shadows dance in dappled light.

Woven in Lavender Hues

In fields of purple, laughter's found,
Where petals mingle, joy unbound.
Bees wear crowns of pollen dust,
In this sweet spot, it's a must.

A ladybug spins like a top,
While butterflies do the funny hop.
Lavender scents float in between,
Each giggle hints at a fun scene.

Stalks of thyme play leap and bound,
Amidst the blooms, joy's tightly wound.
They chuckle soft in the warm sun,
Nature's chorus of silly fun.

Each bloom a heart that softly sings,
Wrapped in sweetness, joy it brings.
With colors bright and scents so free,
This garden is a comedy!

Lyrical Lilacs

In lilac lanes where laughter roams,
Petals dance, a silly dome.
The bumblebees, they start to sway,
Telling jokes in a buzzing way.

Each blossom nods with glee and pride,
As friendly hues start to collide.
The sunshine beams, all smiles around,
In this parade of playful sound.

A joke from the wind makes flowers laugh,
Turning leaves into a comic staff.
With every gust, the petals prance,
Inviting all to join the dance.

An echo of joy fills the air,
In shades of purple, beyond compare.
In this whimsical floral domain,
Laughter and blooms shall ever reign.

The Allure of the Canopy

In the branches up high, birds flap,
Sipping sweet nectar, it's quite a trap.
They giggle and chirp, I cringe with a sigh,
As the squirrels gather nuts, way up in the sky.

Frogs wear their hats, as they jump on the grass,
Wishing to blend in, but they're quite the sass.
They dance in a circle, oh what a sight,
While I try not to laugh, in the morning light.

Bees buzzing loudly, they're quite the loud crew,
They tease each other, "Hey, I'm cuter than you!"
But no one seems bothered, it's all in good fun,
In the shades of the leaves, under the sun.

Oh, what a wonder, this canopy cheer,
Where laughter is planted, and joy grows near.
Nature's own circus, a delightful spree,
In the green, wild world, just waiting for me.

The Garden Muse

Petunias are plotting, oh what a scheme,
While tulips in tutus dance in a dream.
They gossip and giggle, about who wears it best,
In the wonderful garden, where joy's a fest.

The carrots are chatting, with radishes bold,
"Have you heard the stories that garlic has told?"
They share their green stories, all twinkling with glee,
While lettuce rolls over, in fits of green glee.

The sunflowers sway, like they're keeping a beat,
Joining in laughter, with their roots on the street.
A garden of jesters, adorned in their hues,
Bringing smiles to faces, that's my kind of muse.

Whispers of petals, and rustles of leaves,
All sing together, with giggles and heaves.
In this jolly patch, where humor is king,
The garden's my home, where we dance and we sing.

Odes of the Orchard

In the orchard of laughter, the apples confer,
"Who's the juiciest?" they giggle, with a purr.
Peaches roll in, all fuzzy and bright,
While cherries titter softly, "Who can take flight?"

The pears play a game, they're hiding away,
But the prunes always win, it's their favorite play.
With whispers to branches, they giggle anew,
As the breezes come tickling, just like they do.

Ripe berries are jesters, with jokes on the vine,
"Have you heard the one, of the grape's favorite line?"
They chuckle together, under shade's friendly hold,
In this orchard of fun, where stories unfold.

Each fruit finds a friend, in the warm sun's glow,
A harmony sweet, where the laughter does flow.
With roots in the soil, and hearts full of cheer,
The odes of our orchard, bring giggles near.

Sibilant Stems

Sibilant stems whisper, secrets to buds,
Telling tales of rustling, and chill of the floods.
With a wink and a sway, they giggle so tight,
As the garden laughs back, with all of its might.

The zany zinnias dance, twirling 'round fast,
While daisies just shake, as they're stuck in the past.
"Catch us if you can!" shouts the playful green,
In the shimmery shadows, where joy's often seen.

Vines laced in laughter, they twist and they twine,
Bamboos do a jig, while the sunbeams align.
In the quirky bouquet, where giggles parade,
The sibilant stems sing with joy that won't fade.

With petals in gossip, and laughter on leaves,
Nature's own humor, is what each one believes.
In this fun-filled domain, where whimsy takes root,
The tales of the stems, always keep it astute.

Gardening with Stanzas

In the garden, vibes are great,
The flowers sing, let's celebrate.
Bees dance around with a little buzz,
While a squirrel steals a plant with a fuss.

We planted seeds, a colorful spree,
But things went wild, oh can't you see?
Carrots popped up, sticking out their heads,
And pumpkins rolled like sleepy beds.

The rake's a wand, I wave it right,
To chase away weeds, what a silly sight!
Laughter echoes through sunny days,
As I trip on roots in a playful haze.

So gather round, let's plant and play,
In our garden, fun's here to stay.
With each new sprout, life's absurd,
In this quirky world, joy's unblurred.

Verses In Full Bloom

In the garden plot, I set my scene,
Weeds look at me, and give a sheen.
They wave their leaves, a sneaky prank,
While I try to dig, my pants fall frank.

The sun shines down, it's warming me,
But where's my hat? It's on a tree!
A chipmunk giggles, all while he steals,
My precious seeds—he surely feels!

Grabbing the hose, thoughts go astray,
Water goes up, down, all over the way.
Squeezed by the nozzle, I dance, I twirl,
As a puddle forms and chaos unfurl.

So raise a cheer for blooms so bright,
For the laughter shared in morning light.
Gardening dreams, all tangled and wild,
In this funny patch, I'm nature's child.

Garden of Stanzas

In my patch of green, mischief is sprout,
Daisies and tulips dance about.
Rabbits hop in with a cheeky grin,
While I chase them, oh where to begin!

With watering cans, we march in line,
A brigade of plants, oh aren't they fine?
But wait! A snail joins, moves slow as glue,
I think he likes my hat, what's he gonna do?

Sunflowers tower, like guards of the sun,
And I'm tangled up—oh what a run!
A butterfly lands, takes a little nap,
On my nose, oh what a floral trap!

So join the fun in this garden-bound spree,
With laughter and blooms, it's wild and free.
Together we play, in a world so spry,
Amidst the flowers, we'll laugh and sigh.

Fragile Whispers

In the gentle breeze, whispers are light,
Petals giggle as they take flight.
A bumblebee swoops, oh what a sight,
It tickles my nose, and starts a fight!

Swinging my spade like a knight of old,
I battle with weeds, so proud and bold.
But oh dear me, they just won't quit,
Their feisty dance, quite a comedy skit!

With muck on my shoes, I waddle along,
The garden's a stage, our hearts are a song.
As daffodils nod, and violets beam,
We burst out laughing, it seems like a dream.

So here's to the fun in our flowered space,
With giggles and grins, life's a sweet race.
In the garden's embrace, we find our tune,
With every bud's bloom, we all are in swoon.

Lyricism of Leaves

In the garden, they dance and twirl,
Colors bright, in a leafy swirl.
They whisper secrets, tickle my nose,
Giggling softly, as the breeze blows.

Each petal a note, each bud a laugh,
Nature's own silly photograph.
They play hide and seek with the bees,
Chasing shadows, feeling the breeze.

With laughter loud, they sway and swing,
A silly symphony, they all bring.
Flapping their petals like tiny wings,
In the sunlight, joyfully sings.

So come and join this leafy spree,
Where the plant life has a grand jubilee!
Friends and flowers, sharing delight,
Under the sun, all feels just right.

Stanzas in Shades of Green

In tattered hats, they're all in line,
Wiggling around like it's all fine.
With every flutter, giggles arise,
Tickled by sunlight and blue skies.

A leafy lunch, they seem to host,
While insects perform a comedic roast.
They poke and prod, oh what a sight,
Nature's comedy, pure delight!

And when rain falls, they splash and play,
Making puddles in a joyful ballet.
All around, the mischief flows,
As nature's funny side surely shows.

So gather 'round, let laughter bloom,
In this green theater where joy finds room.
With every leaf, a smile unrolls,
As the sun winks at nature's goals.

Blooming in Silence

In the stillness, petals peek,
With cheeky grins, they softly speak.
They burst out laughing, loud and bright,
In their secret world, pure delight.

With silent jokes and subtle jests,
They play their game, their very best.
In hues of whimsy, they create a show,
Where quiet giggles and colors flow.

They shimmy and shake, as if to tease,
Prompting chuckles from buzzing bees.
A silent dance, a muted cheer,
In the quiet, hilarity draws near.

Oh, to join their subtle spree,
In the shadows, where all's carefree!
For in their blooms, humor thrives,
In nature's laughter, joy arrives.

A Symphony of Sights

In a chorus of colors, they splash and sway,
With petals that giggle in a zany display.
Every bud is a note, every bloom a tune,
Composing a melody beneath the moon.

They rustle like pages in a storybook,
Inviting all passersby to stop and look.
Playing the lead in this whimsical show,
With their playful antics, they steal the glow.

A jam session erupts with each gust of breeze,
Tickling the branches and teasing the leaves.
Nature's orchestra, wild and free,
Creating a laughter-filled symphony.

So here's to the petals that love to play,
In a world where silliness lights up the day.
Join these blooms in their joyful flight,
In the symphony of sights, everything's bright!

Serenity in the Stem

In gardens where the colors sing,
A flower dreams of just one thing:
To dance with bees from dawn till dusk,
And never fear a bit of musk.

With leaves that stretch, as if to tease,
It wiggles in the gentle breeze.
"I'm not a weed, just look at me!"
Says every sprout with glee and glee.

Where shades of pink and purple blend,
They giggle like a blooming friend.
In every pot, a story's told,
Of sunlight's warmth and raindrops bold.

So when you walk those garden lanes,
Just laugh along with leafy gains.
For every petal that you see,
Is just a joke from nature's spree.

Petals of the Past

Once spoke a bud so young and spry,
"I heard a rumor, don't ask me why!"
It claimed that roots could tell a tale,
   Of snails who wore a tiny sail.

With petals bright, it shimmies low,
And whispers secrets soft and slow.
"Yesterday's sunshine was the best,
   But now I fancy a garden fest!"

The blooms all giggle, full of cheer,
As clumsy spiders dance near here.
"I tripped again!" one spider cried,
As petals tucked their laughter wide.

And with each breeze, the flowers sway,
   Sharing memories from yesterday.
   It's funny how they hold on tight,
   To tales of joy, both day and night.

Blooming Verses

In every corner, colors shout,
Each blossom quests to find a sprout.
"I'm the best!" the yellow cries,
While purple rolls its silly eyes.

They plan a party, brightly bold,
With petals dressed in stories told.
The daffodil brings lemon slices,
While daisies dance with rolling vices.

Beneath the blooms, the bugs all cheer,
With tiny hats and jokes sincere.
"Let's feast on nectar, sing and play,
And celebrate this sunny day!"

So laugh aloud when flowers bloom,
They Plotting joy in nature's room.
For every giggle, twist, and twirl,
Is just a party, oh what a whirl!

Petals of Versatility

A flower claimed, "I've got the knack,
To wear a hat, or even a pack!"
It twirled and swayed in sunlight's hue,
While others just laughed, as flowers do.

"I'm more than pretty," said the rose,
"I can be a dancer, just watch my pose!"
The daisies giggled, "We're cheerleaders bright,
Let's show the world our blooming might!"

With every petal, each one thinks,
Of silly pranks and juicy winks.
The tulip rolled its eyes with glee,
"I'm the funniest flower, can't you see?"

So if you wander through their bliss,
Just stop and share a blooming kiss.
For in the garden, joy's the key,
As every flower sings with glee!

Lines of the Leaf

In the garden, leaves take a twirl,
Dancing gently, giving a whirl.
One leaf asked the other, with glee,
"Have you seen my cousin, the bumblebee?"

They laughed as the breeze gave a shove,
"We're the original tree's hand-dove!"
"When people come to sniff and stare,
Let's play hide and seek; we'll disappear into thin air!"

With colors bright, they felt like kings,
Swinging about on invisible strings.
The sun peeked down, bright and slick,
"Watch this dance! It'll make you tick!"

The flowers giggled, sharing a wink,
"Have you heard the latest on that pink?"
Petals swirling, making a fuss,
While plump bugs waddle on the bus.

Enchanted Blooms

In a patch of laughter, flowers bloom,
With poky stems, they banish gloom.
A daisy cried, "I'm just too cute!"
While roses sighed, "What's with the loot?"

A playful breeze tickled their petals,
"Dance, oh dance," sang the silly metals!
With a swirl of colors bright and jolly,
The daisies burst, in a giggly folly.

"Do you feel the sun's warm hug?"
A tulip grinned, giving a shrug.
"I'll tell you a secret, just between us:
This land is ours, let's make a fuss!"

They chirped and cheered in the cheerful vein,
As gossip spread like summer rain.
"Who wore it better, the lilac or me?"
"Well, I'd say it depends on the bee!"

Ephemeral Expressions

Petals prance with vibrant flair,
Whispering tales with fragrant air.
A blooming bud chuckled in delight,
"Hold on tight, it's quite a sight!"

The daisies waved a friendly hello,
As butterflies put on a show.
"If you think you can outshine my hue,
You better bring a deck of cards too!"

In the garden of giggles and play,
Blooming flowers brighten the day.
They told each other when to shine,
"No need to rush, we'll be just fine!"

A daffodil winked, a simple tease,
"Why hold back? Let's dance with ease!"
And in that moment, under the sun,
The field exploded with joy, oh what fun!

"Our colors laugh, our smells combine,
This garden's magic is purely divine!"
As shadows stretched, and the day took a bow,
The flowers grinned, "Let's take a vow!"

The Imprint of Flora

In a whimsically wild little glade,
Florescent blooms have got it made.
With chubby petals and silly sways,
They toast to laughter in sunny rays!

A jaunt in the garden, oh what a treat,
As flowers gossip and wiggle their feet.
"Who left the dirt on my new dress?"
"Never mind, let's just say it's excess!"

The tulips laughed, in shades so slick,
"Watch out now, I feel a trick!"
With a puff and a giggle, they bounced with ease,
Creating stories in the rustling breeze.

"Did you hear the one about the tree?"
"He thought he could dance, but he stumbled with glee!"
And so the blooms burst into a fit,
In their funny storybook, where laughter is lit.

The Canvas of Blooms

In a garden bright and zany,
The flowers dance, quite insane-y.
Petals twirl in vibrant glee,
Hoping birds will sing with me.

Bees buzz by with a silly grin,
Wearing pollen like a win-win.
Bunnies hop, do a funny jig,
Chasing butterflies, oh so big!

A scarecrow cracks a goofy joke,
While the daffodils just choke.
Laughter echoes through the air,
As squirrels plot their nutty dare.

The sun winks down on this funny show,
Creating joy that starts to grow.
In this canvas, colors collide,
A whimsical world, let's take a ride!

Harmonies of the Garden

In the gardens where we play,
Flowers sing both night and day.
Tulips boast their golden hues,
While daisies gossip with the blues.

A gnome tunes in with his flute,
Singing to the roots and shoot.
The roses chuckle, oh what fun,
As petunias join in, one by one.

Worms are dancing in the soil,
Planning pranks, no sign of toil.
Even crickets join the beat,
Making this a grand retreat.

With a bounce and a little cheer,
All the blooms draw each one near.
In harmony, they spin and sway,
Turning every frown to play!

Vibrant Verse

In a garden full of flair,
Every blossom has a dare.
Pansies wear the silliest hats,
While sunflowers chat with chatty bats.

Petals flutter like a jacket,
With colors bright, oh what a racket!
Nasturtiums giggle as they bloom,
Filling the air with a sweet perfume.

A clever frog starts to croon,
Ribbits dancing to the tune.
With the breeze playing along,
Nature's heart sings a witty song.

This rhyming garden blooms with fun,
Where laughter sparkles in the sun.
Join the frolic, don't be shy,
In this vibrant verse, we'll fly high!

Blossoming Sonnet

In a blossom realm, the giggles rise,
Petals wave like cheerful spies.
A funnyman bee starts to jest,
While daisies giggle, feeling blessed.

Birds chirp puns in feathered tunes,
Tickling leaves, shaking the moons.
Tulips blush a rosy hue,
As violets blush, oh so true!

The sun plays hide and seek with shade,
While ants parade in a grand parade.
With every stem bending low,
The garden echoes joy's sweet flow.

So gather round, let laughter bloom,
In this bright, enchanting room.
With petals' joy that spins and sways,
In our blossoming sonnet, let's play!

A Tapestry of Colors

In a garden bright, oh what a scene,
Pink and purple, like a paint magazine.
Bees in tuxedos, buzzing around,
Dancing with petals where laughter is found.

Silly little buds, wobbling with glee,
Winking at sunshine, waving to me.
They gossip and giggle in soft, breezy air,
Promises of nectar, sweetness to share.

The sun slips away, but they don't mind it,
Colorful clowns in a floral cast fit.
Tomorrow they'll sparkle, in nature's own play,
A tapestry woven, in wild, happy sway.

The Blooming Narrative

Once upon a stem, a tale took root,
A flower's bold journey, sprouting with loot.
Chasing the drizzle, all dressed up fine,
Mistakes made in petals can lead to divine.

Oh, how they chuckle, the blooms so spry,
Telling their stories to passerby.
Colors collide in playful daze,
Creating a laughter that simply amaze.

A daffodil joked, "I've got the best sun!"
While daisies chimed in, "Oh, this is just fun!"
With bees as their band, they danced down the lane,
A blooming narrative that drives us insane.

Singing with Blossoms

Blossoms in choir, what a delightful group,
Singing in harmony, a nature's grand troupe.
Jokers with petals and smiles on their face,
Mischief in pollen, creating a trace.

"Hey there, snapdragon, why the long face?"
"Just waiting for beetles to join the fun race."
The lilac laughed loudly, all joy and cheer,
While the tulips twirled, "Our season is here!"

In hilarious airtime, they frolic and sway,
Telling their secrets in flowers' bouquet.
With roots intertwined, they banter and croon,
Singing with blossoms, beneath the soft moon.

Ink and Petals

A splash of ink, on a petal's soft glow,
Sketching little stories in nature's tableau.
With quills made of thorns, they scribble and laugh,
Rendering petals as a comedic path.

Whispers in watercolor, they giggle and tease,
Painting the air, like a light summer breeze.
"Did you hear my joke?" a tulip will say,
"To bloom in full color, brightens the day!"

The bees scribe verses, buzzing on the fly,
Prints of sweet humor where flowers sigh.
In vibrant hues, they dance with delight,
Ink and petals unite, in the warm twilight.

The Language of Leaves

The leaves gossip in the breeze,
Whispering secrets from the trees.
They chuckle and giggle, oh so sly,
As squirrels dance and rabbits pry.

Each rustle holds a playful jest,
Nature's laughing, feeling blessed.
A leaf winks, a branch will sway,
Who knew plants could be this gay?

In green attire, they twist and twine,
Telling tales of sun and wine.
Their laughter echoes through the glade,
In leafy games, they're unafraid.

So join the chatter, hear the cheer,
In this leafy world, there's no fear.
With every rustle, a silly tease,
In the forest of giggles, we all freeze.

Nature's Chorus

A chorus rings from flowered boughs,
Singing loud with cheerful vows.
Bees buzzing in off-key tones,
While daisies dance on wobbly stones.

In harmony, they sway and sway,
A kooky tune in bright array.
The tulips clap with petals wide,
As butterflies lead the merry ride.

Laughter blooms where the wild things play,
Nature's jesters on display.
Each note a chuckle, each laugh a hue,
Come join the fun; it's a lively crew!

So tiptoe softly through the bloom,
And catch a smile in every room.
In this nature's band, let joy perfume,
A funny tune will always loom!

Floral Reflections

Look at the flowers in the sun,
Giggling brightly, oh what fun!
They chat in colors, bold and grand,
Waving to bugs with a gentle hand.

Petal faces make a scene,
Poking fun at what's pristine.
With laughter painted in each hue,
They giggle secrets, just us two.

A daffodil's joke, a rose's grin,
What's the punchline? Where to begin!
They play hide-and-seek with the breeze,
Finding humor in giggling trees.

Mirror, mirror, on the field,
What funny stories will you yield?
In floral laughter, joy reflects,
In every petal, joy connects.

The Palette of Spring

Spring splashes colors, oh what a sight,
With shades that giggle from morning to night.
The blossoms tease in yellows and pinks,
While trees don green and share their winks.

Hues collide in a playful jest,
Nature's chaos, truly the best!
In every brushstroke, laughs unfold,
Like jokes in the air, bright and bold.

A lilac giggles, a tulip shrieks,
Crafting laughter in vibrant peaks.
Carnations frolic, with petals bright,
Creating a canvas of pure delight.

So sharpen your eyes for this joyful spree,
In spring's palette, we're wild and free.
Join the artists, let's laugh and sing,
As we celebrate the joy of spring!

Notes from the Garden

In the garden, plants do jig,
With the worms that dance a gig.
Bees buzz in their silly flight,
While blossoms giggle with delight.

Sunflowers wear their hats so wide,
Daffodils play peek-a-boo with pride.
The carrots grumble underground,
As cabbage rolls are tumbling 'round.

Tulips gossip with the breeze,
Telling tales with such great ease.
Lilies laugh, they flip and flop,
While daisies never want to stop.

Oh, what fun this garden brings,
Where veggies dance and nature sings.
Join the riot, leave your cares,
In this place, joy is everywhere!

The Verse of Violets

Violets blush in shades of blue,
Tickled by the morning dew.
They wear their petals like a crown,
And chuckle as the insects frown.

Bumblebees join in the fun,
Buzzing round just like a run.
"Oh look!" the violets tease and play,
"We're the stars of the bright, fine day!"

The wind whispers silly jokes,
As the daisies throw little pokes.
Each bloom a comedian on the stage,
With petals like a silly page.

At sunset, violets close their eyes,
As crickets share their night-time sighs.
A symphony of laughs abound,
In this garden, joy is found!

Colorful Chronicles

In patches bright, the colors flare,
A canvas fresh, beyond compare.
Each hue a character so bold,
With secrets rich and tales untold.

Roses wearing a dazzling smile,
Pose like actors with great style.
Nasturtiums giggle, spill their tea,
While ferns sway in harmony.

Pansies pull their pranky stunts,
Every petal holding laughs in bunches.
Lilac scents the air so sweet,
As blooms break into dance and beat.

Every garden tells a tale,
Of flowered friends that never fail.
Join their fun, embrace the cheer,
In colorful tales, we hold so dear!

Where Blooms Speak

In the meadow, flowers chitchat,
Sun-kissed petals in bright format.
"Who has the silliest hat?" they muse,
While butterflies play peek-a-boo blues.

The marigolds boast of their flair,
While sunflowers claim they're the best for air.
"Don't forget our colors," they cry,
As violets wink their sparkles high.

Dandelions laugh at the breeze,
As poppies drop their petals with ease.
"Oh, what a jolly bunch!" they sing,
In the garden, joy is king!

When twilight falls, they hum a tune,
Beneath the gaze of the sweet moon.
In this place where blooms do speak,
Each petal shines, each laugh unique!

www.ingramcontent.com/pod-product-compliance
Lightning Source LLC
Chambersburg PA
CBHW070751220426
43209CB00083B/403